THIS READING LOG BELONGS TO

IF LOST, PLEASE CONTACT ME AT:

DEDICATION

This Reading Log is dedicated to all the readers out there who love to read and document their findings in the process.

You are my inspiration for producing books and I'm honored to be a part of keeping all of your Reading notes and records organized.

This journal notebook will help you record your details about tracking the time you spent reading.

Thoughtfully put together with these sections to record: Date, Title of the Book, Pages Read, and Review Rating.

HOW TO USE THIS BOOK

The purpose of this book is to keep all of your Reading Log notes all in one place. It will help keep you organized.

This Reading Log Book will allow you to accurately document every detail about your books and pages read.

Here are examples of the prompts for you to fill in and write about your experience in this book:

1. Date

2. Title

3. Pages Read

4. Review Rating

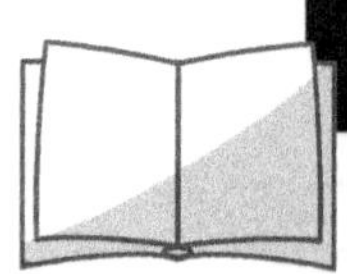

READING LOG

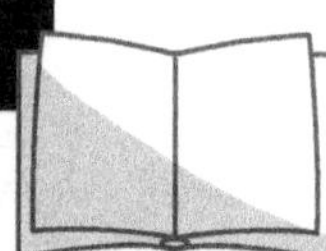

DATE	TITLE OF BOOK	PAGES READ	RATING 1-5

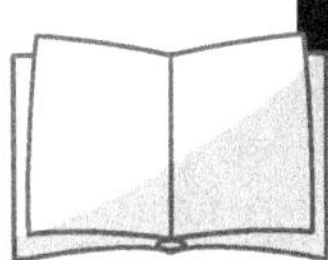

READING LOG

DATE	TITLE OF BOOK	PAGES READ	RATING 1-5

READING LOG

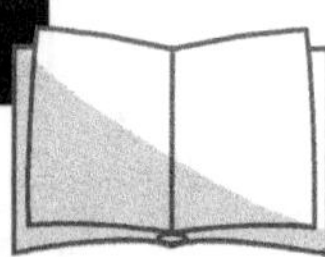

DATE	TITLE OF BOOK	PAGES READ	RATING 1-5

READING LOG

DATE	TITLE OF BOOK	PAGES READ	RATING 1-5

READING LOG

DATE	TITLE OF BOOK	PAGES READ	RATING 1-5

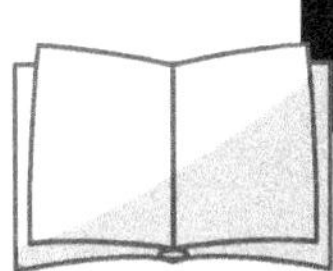

READING LOG

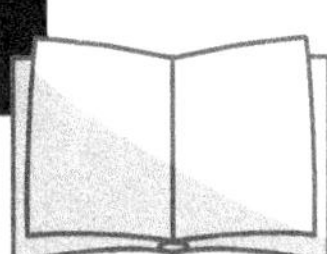

DATE	TITLE OF BOOK	PAGES READ	RATING 1-5

READING LOG

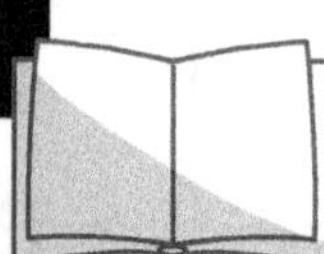

DATE	TITLE OF BOOK	PAGES READ	RATING 1-5

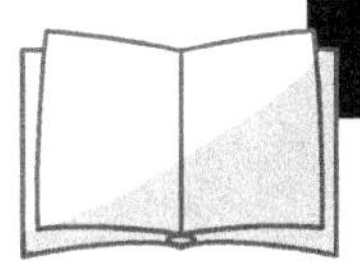

READING LOG

DATE	TITLE OF BOOK	PAGES READ	RATING 1-5

READING LOG

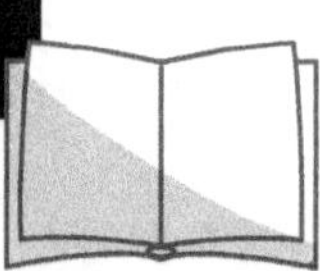

DATE	TITLE OF BOOK	PAGES READ	RATING 1-5

READING LOG

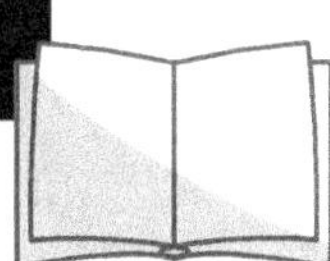

DATE	TITLE OF BOOK	PAGES READ	RATING 1-5

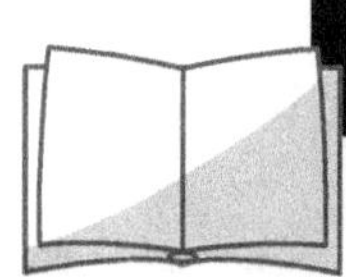

READING LOG

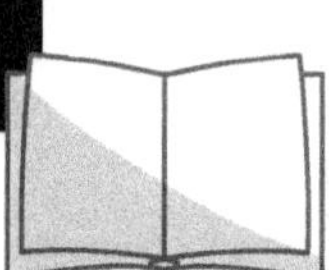

DATE	TITLE OF BOOK	PAGES READ	RATING 1-5

READING LOG

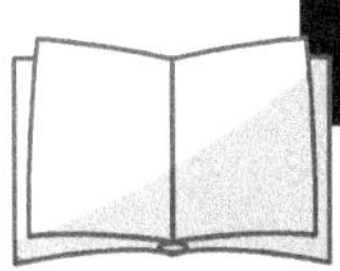
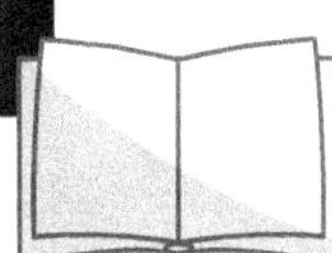

DATE	TITLE OF BOOK	PAGES READ	RATING 1-5

READING LOG

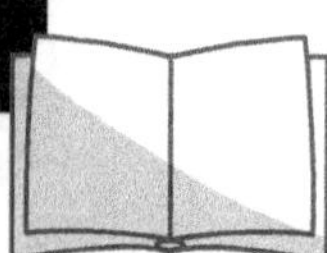

DATE	TITLE OF BOOK	PAGES READ	RATING 1-5

READING LOG

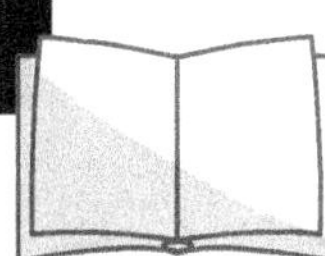

DATE	TITLE OF BOOK	PAGES READ	RATING 1-5

READING LOG

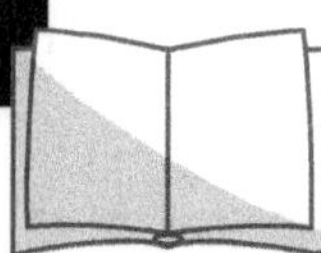

DATE	TITLE OF BOOK	PAGES READ	RATING 1-5

READING LOG

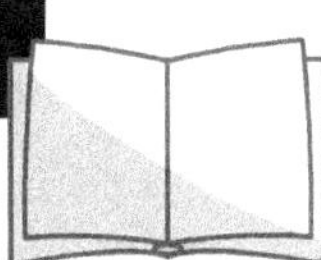

DATE	TITLE OF BOOK	PAGES READ	RATING 1-5

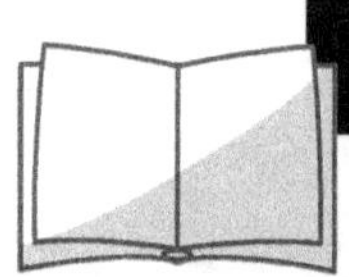

READING LOG

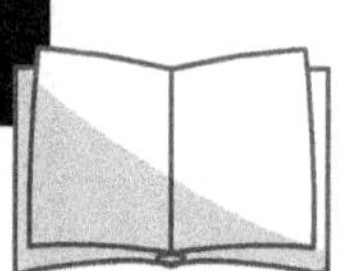

DATE	TITLE OF BOOK	PAGES READ	RATING 1-5

READING LOG

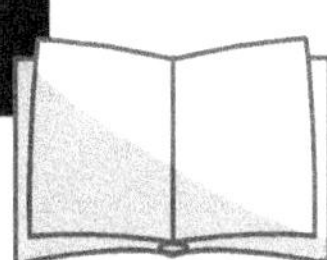

DATE	TITLE OF BOOK	PAGES READ	RATING 1-5

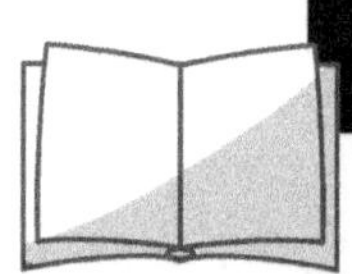

READING LOG

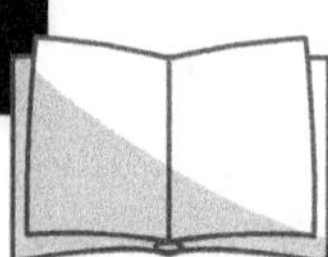

DATE	TITLE OF BOOK	PAGES READ	RATING 1-5

READING LOG

DATE	TITLE OF BOOK	PAGES READ	RATING 1-5

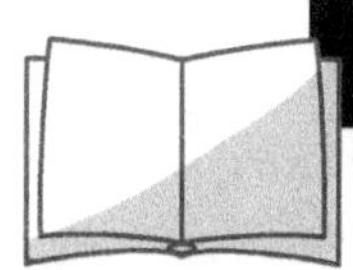

READING LOG

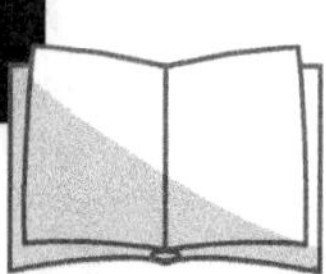

DATE	TITLE OF BOOK	PAGES READ	RATING 1-5

READING LOG

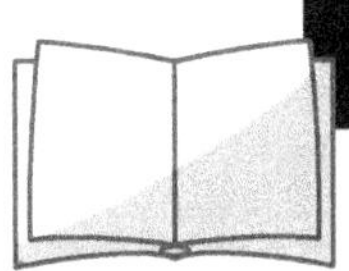
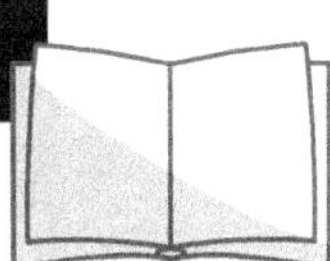

DATE	TITLE OF BOOK	PAGES READ	RATING 1-5

READING LOG

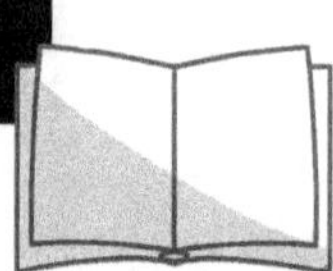

DATE	TITLE OF BOOK	PAGES READ	RATING 1-5

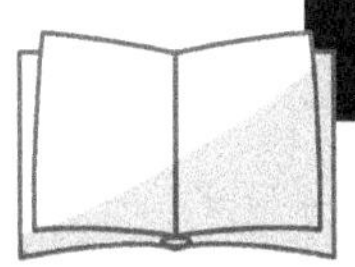

READING LOG

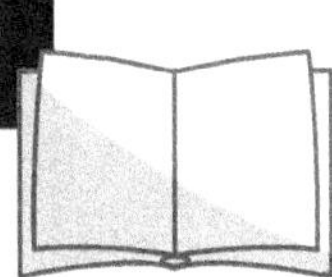

DATE	TITLE OF BOOK	PAGES READ	RATING 1-5

READING LOG

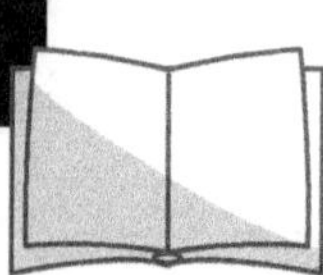

DATE	TITLE OF BOOK	PAGES READ	RATING 1-5

READING LOG

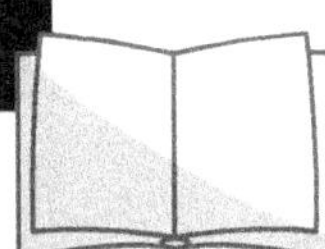

DATE	TITLE OF BOOK	PAGES READ	RATING 1-5

READING LOG

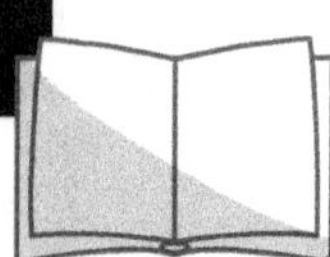

DATE	TITLE OF BOOK	PAGES READ	RATING 1-5

READING LOG

DATE	TITLE OF BOOK	PAGES READ	RATING 1-5

READING LOG

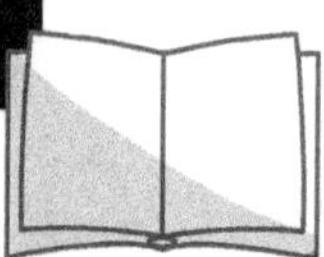

DATE	TITLE OF BOOK	PAGES READ	RATING 1-5

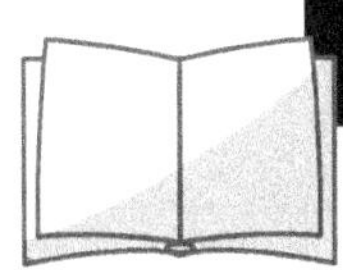

READING LOG

DATE	TITLE OF BOOK	PAGES READ	RATING 1-5

READING LOG

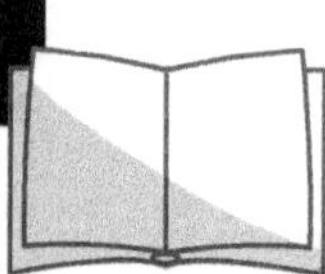

DATE	TITLE OF BOOK	PAGES READ	RATING 1-5

READING LOG

DATE	TITLE OF BOOK	PAGES READ	RATING 1-5

READING LOG

DATE	TITLE OF BOOK	PAGES READ	RATING 1-5

READING LOG

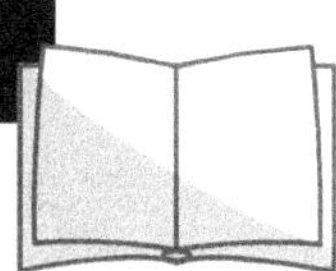

DATE	TITLE OF BOOK	PAGES READ	RATING 1-5

READING LOG

DATE	TITLE OF BOOK	PAGES READ	RATING 1-5

READING LOG

DATE	TITLE OF BOOK	PAGES READ	RATING 1-5

READING LOG

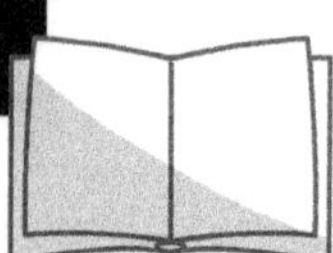

DATE	TITLE OF BOOK	PAGES READ	RATING 1-5

READING LOG

DATE	TITLE OF BOOK	PAGES READ	RATING 1-5

READING LOG

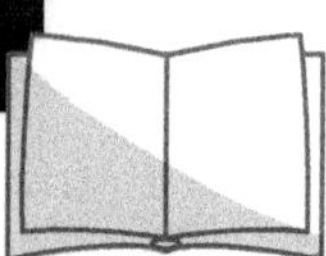

DATE	TITLE OF BOOK	PAGES READ	RATING 1-5

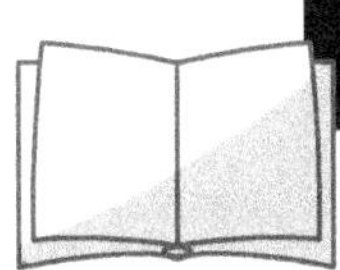

READING LOG

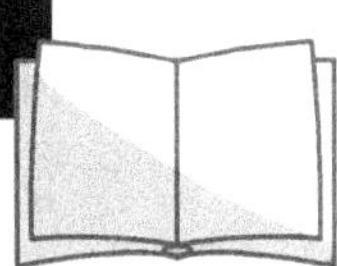

DATE	TITLE OF BOOK	PAGES READ	RATING 1-5

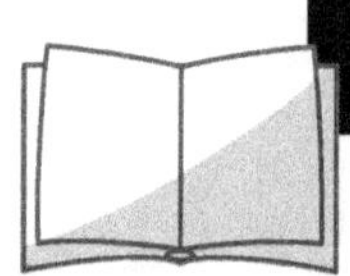

READING LOG

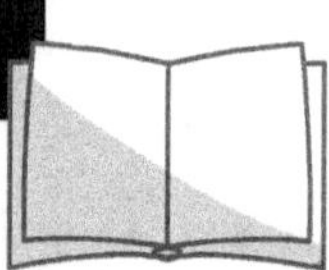

DATE	TITLE OF BOOK	PAGES READ	RATING 1-5

READING LOG

DATE	TITLE OF BOOK	PAGES READ	RATING 1-5

READING LOG

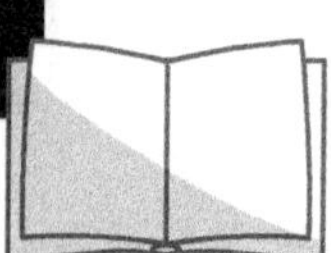

DATE	TITLE OF BOOK	PAGES READ	RATING 1-5

READING LOG

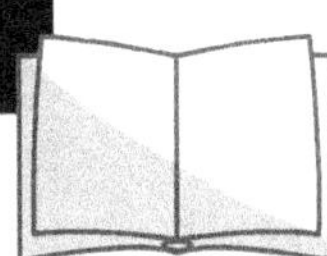

DATE	TITLE OF BOOK	PAGES READ	RATING 1-5

READING LOG

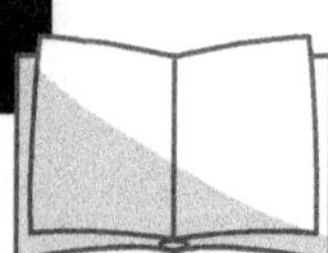

DATE	TITLE OF BOOK	PAGES READ	RATING 1-5

READING LOG

DATE	TITLE OF BOOK	PAGES READ	RATING 1-5

READING LOG

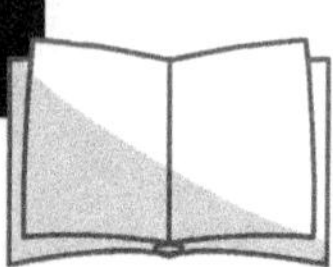

DATE	TITLE OF BOOK	PAGES READ	RATING 1-5

READING LOG

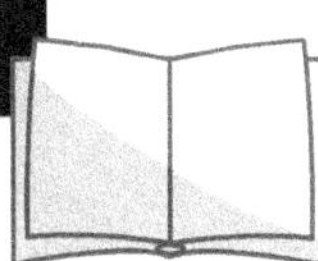

DATE	TITLE OF BOOK	PAGES READ	RATING 1-5

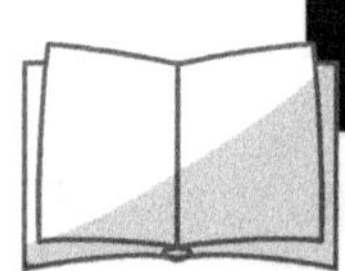

READING LOG

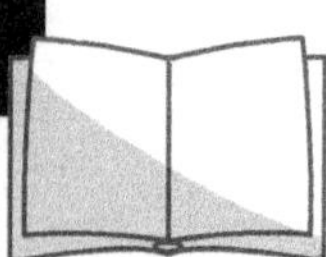

DATE	TITLE OF BOOK	PAGES READ	RATING 1-5

READING LOG

DATE	TITLE OF BOOK	PAGES READ	RATING 1-5

READING LOG

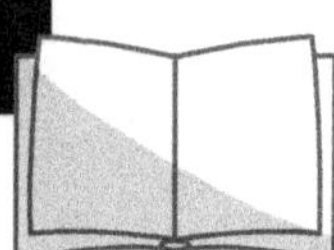

DATE	TITLE OF BOOK	PAGES READ	RATING 1-5

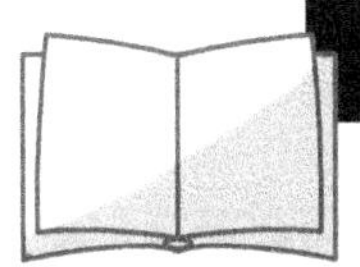

READING LOG

DATE	TITLE OF BOOK	PAGES READ	RATING 1-5

READING LOG

DATE	TITLE OF BOOK	PAGES READ	RATING 1-5

READING LOG

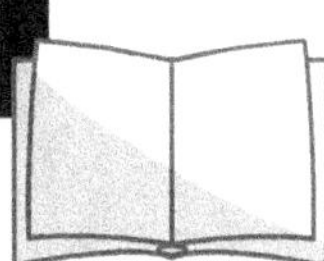

DATE	TITLE OF BOOK	PAGES READ	RATING 1-5

READING LOG

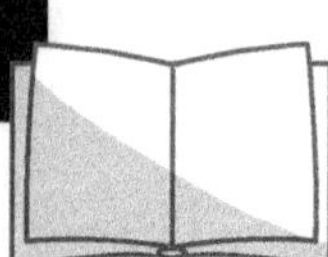

DATE	TITLE OF BOOK	PAGES READ	RATING 1-5

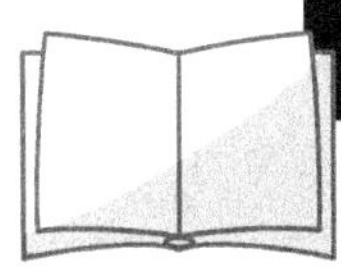

READING LOG

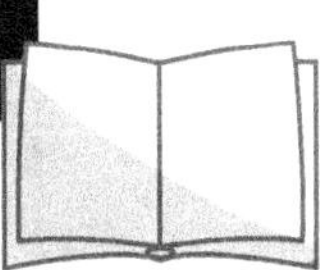

DATE	TITLE OF BOOK	PAGES READ	RATING 1-5

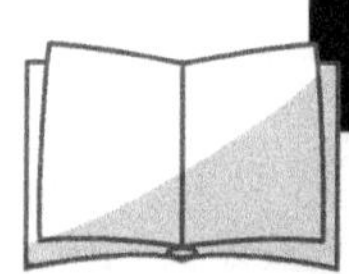

READING LOG

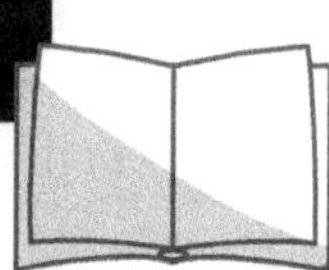

DATE	TITLE OF BOOK	PAGES READ	RATING 1-5

READING LOG

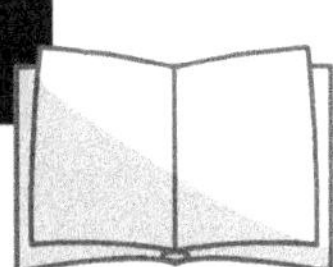

DATE	TITLE OF BOOK	PAGES READ	RATING 1-5

READING LOG

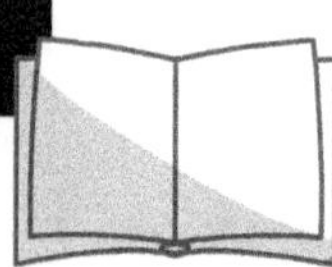

DATE	TITLE OF BOOK	PAGES READ	RATING 1-5

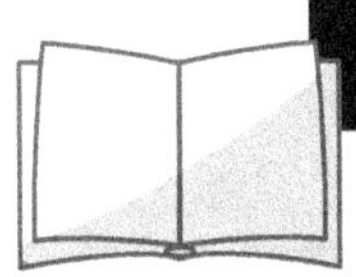

READING LOG

DATE	TITLE OF BOOK	PAGES READ	RATING 1-5

READING LOG

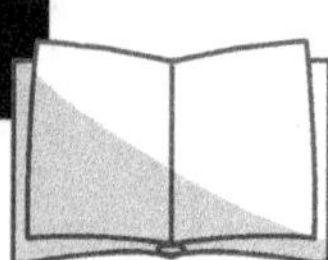

DATE	TITLE OF BOOK	PAGES READ	RATING 1-5

READING LOG

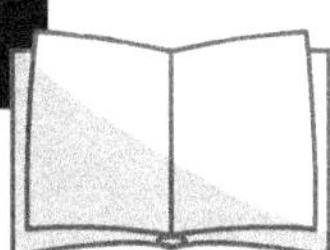

DATE	TITLE OF BOOK	PAGES READ	RATING 1-5

READING LOG

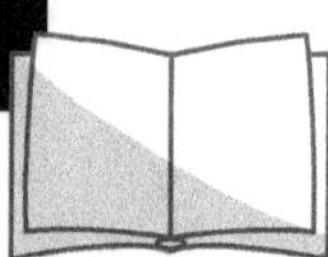

DATE	TITLE OF BOOK	PAGES READ	RATING 1-5

READING LOG

DATE	TITLE OF BOOK	PAGES READ	RATING 1-5

READING LOG

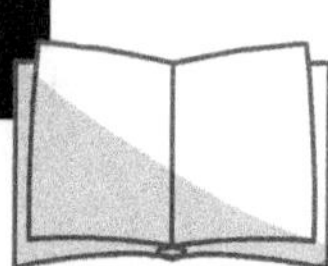

DATE	TITLE OF BOOK	PAGES READ	RATING 1-5

READING LOG

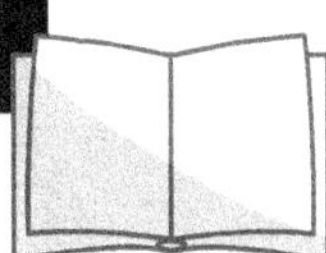

DATE	TITLE OF BOOK	PAGES READ	RATING 1-5

READING LOG

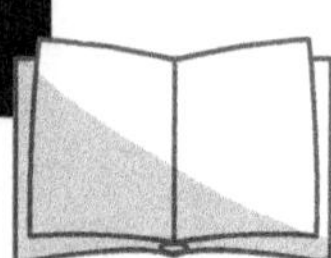

DATE	TITLE OF BOOK	PAGES READ	RATING 1-5

READING LOG

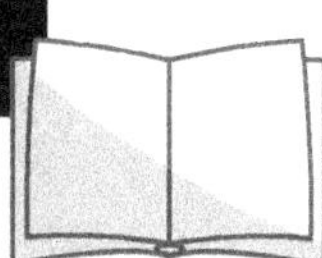

DATE	TITLE OF BOOK	PAGES READ	RATING 1-5

READING LOG

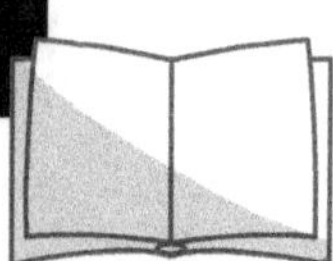

DATE	TITLE OF BOOK	PAGES READ	RATING 1-5

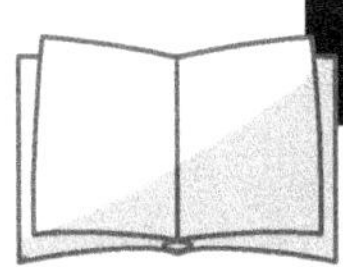

READING LOG

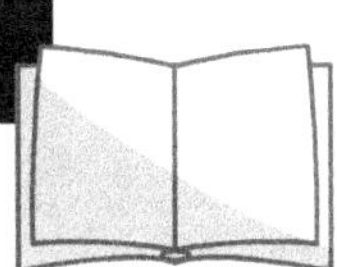

DATE	TITLE OF BOOK	PAGES READ	RATING 1-5

READING LOG

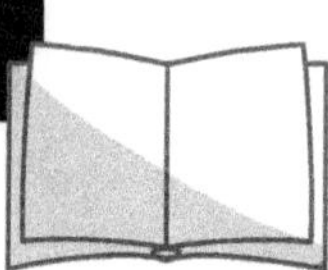

DATE	TITLE OF BOOK	PAGES READ	RATING 1-5

READING LOG

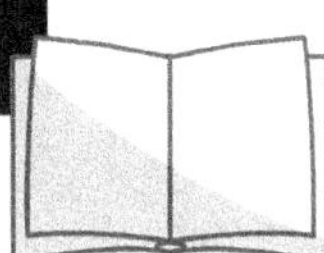

DATE	TITLE OF BOOK	PAGES READ	RATING 1-5

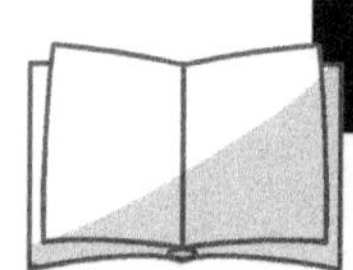

READING LOG

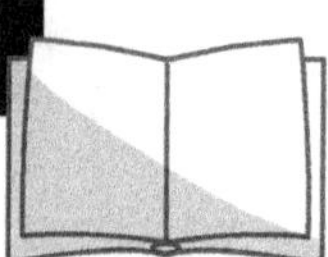

DATE	TITLE OF BOOK	PAGES READ	RATING 1-5

READING LOG

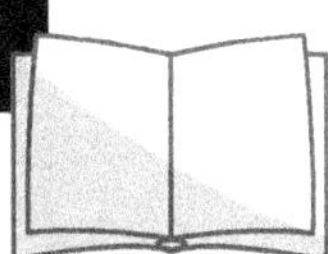

DATE	TITLE OF BOOK	PAGES READ	RATING 1-5

READING LOG

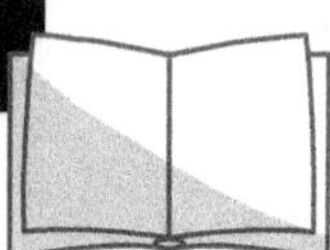

DATE	TITLE OF BOOK	PAGES READ	RATING 1-5

READING LOG

DATE	TITLE OF BOOK	PAGES READ	RATING 1-5

READING LOG

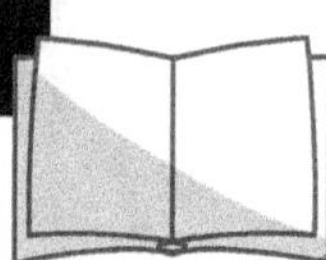

DATE	TITLE OF BOOK	PAGES READ	RATING 1-5

READING LOG

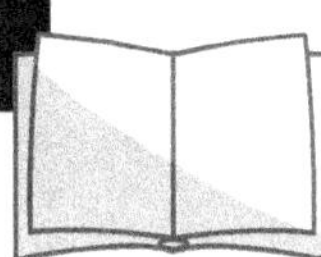

DATE	TITLE OF BOOK	PAGES READ	RATING 1-5

READING LOG

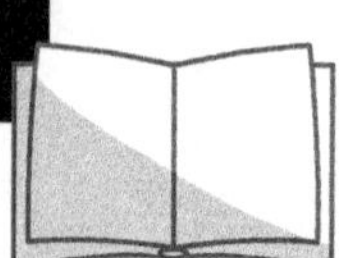

DATE	TITLE OF BOOK	PAGES READ	RATING 1-5

READING LOG

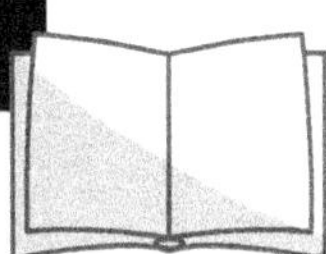

DATE	TITLE OF BOOK	PAGES READ	RATING 1-5

READING LOG

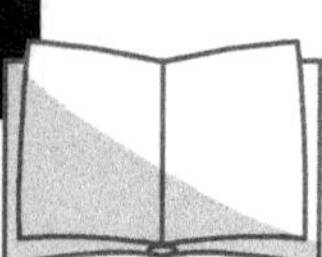

DATE	TITLE OF BOOK	PAGES READ	RATING 1-5

www.ingramcontent.com/pod-product-compliance
Lightning Source LLC
Chambersburg PA
CBHW070913100726
47907CB00008B/2310

* 9 7 8 1 6 4 9 4 4 2 6 9 7 *